BIOGRAPHY FROM
ANCIENT CIVILIZATIONS
LEGENDS, FOLKLORE, AND STORIES OF ANCIENT WORLDS

The Life and Times of

CONFUCIUS

Mitchell Lane
PUBLISHERS

P.O. Box 196
Hockessin, Delaware 19707

Titles
in the Series

The Life and Times of:

BIOGRAPHY FROM
ANCIENT CIVILIZATIONS
LEGENDS, FOLKLORE, AND STORIES OF ANCIENT WORLDS

The Life and Times of

CONFUCIUS

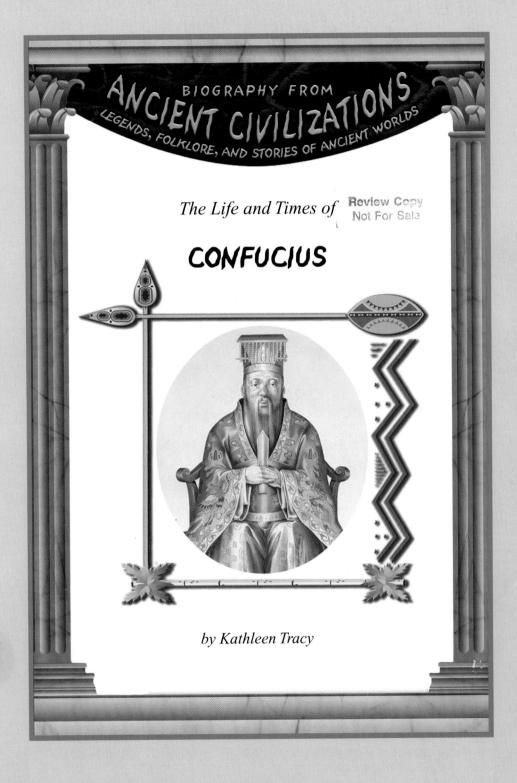

by Kathleen Tracy

Printing 1   2   3   4   5   6   7   8
Library of Congress Cataloging-in-Publication Data

Tracy, Kathleen.
    The life and times of Confucius / Kathleen Tracy.
        p. cm. — (Biography from ancient civilizations)
    Includes bibliographical references (p.   ) and index.
    Contents: The first emperor—A humble beginning—Embracing tradition—The wandering years—An enduring legacy.
    ISBN 1-58415-246-X (lib. bdg.)
    1. Confucius—Juvenile literature. 2. Philosophers—China—Biography—Juvenile literature. [1. Confucius. 2. Philosophers. 3. China—History—To 221 B.C.] I. Title. II. Series.
B128.C8T69 2005
181'.112—dc22

                                                                                2003024050

ABOUT THE AUTHOR: Kathleen Tracy has been a journalist for over twenty years. Her writing has been featured in magazines including *The Toronto Star*'s "Star Week," *A Biography* magazine, *KidScreen* and *TV Times*. She is also the author of numerous biographies including, "The Boy Who Would be King" (Dutton), "Jerry Seinfeld—The Entire Domain" (Carol Publishing), "Don Imus—America's Cowboy" (Carroll), "Mariano Guadalupe Vallejo," and "William Hewlett: Pioneer of the Computer Age," both for Mitchell Lane. She recently completed "God's Will?" for Sourcebooks.

PHOTO CREDITS: Cover, pp. 1, 3, 17, 36—Confucius.org; p. 6—China Page.org; p. 9—Central Union School District/Akers Elementary; p. 12—Maps of China; p. 15—Perdue University; p. 18—Meet-Great Wall.org; p. 18—Chinese News Digest; pp. 20, 26, 36—Minneapolis Institute of Art; p. 23—About the Tao; pp. 24, 28, 34, 40, 41—Corbis; pp. 32, 33—Kevin Atkins; p. 41—Taichung City Cultural Affairs Bureau; p. 41—Synaptic & Grey Matter Media; p. 31—Chinese Culture Net; p. 39—Shippensburg University.

PUBLISHER'S NOTE: This story is based on the author's extensive research, which she believes to be accurate. Documentation of such research is contained on page 47.

The internet sites referenced herein were active as of the publication date. Due to the fleeting nature of some web sites, we cannot guarantee they will all be active when you are reading this book.

BIOGRAPHY FROM
ANCIENT CIVILIZATIONS
LEGENDS, FOLKLORE, AND STORIES OF ANCIENT WORLDS

The Life and Times of

CONFUCIUS

*For Your Information

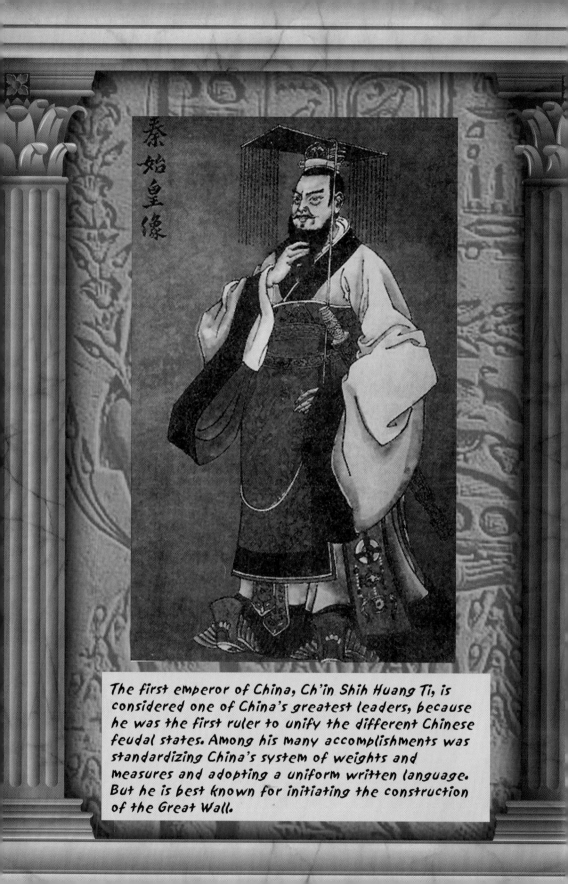

秦始皇像

The first emperor of China, Ch'in Shih Huang Ti, is considered one of China's greatest leaders, because he was the first ruler to unify the different Chinese feudal states. Among his many accomplishments was standardizing China's system of weights and measures and adopting a uniform written language. But he is best known for initiating the construction of the Great Wall.

CHAPTER
ONE

THE FIRST EMPEROR

If you would govern a state of a thousand chariots you must pay strict attention to business, be true to your word, be economical in expenditure and love the people.[1]

In 1974, the area along the Wei River in China was experiencing a drought. The villagers of Xianyang were getting worried because their clean water supply was dwindling. One morning a group of farmers set out to dig a well by the mouth of Wei River near the foot of Mount Lishan. They had been digging for hours when one of the men, Yang Xi Man, felt something hard under the dirt. At first he thought it was simply a buried rock, so he called over to the others to help him dig it out. Instead of stone, they pulled a piece of terra-cotta, or baked clay, out of the ground. It appeared to be a fragment of a warrior figure. Yang Xi Man couldn't have imagined he had just stumbled on the terra-cotta army of Ch'in Shih Huang Ti, the first emperor of China. Considered by many to be the greatest archaeological find of the last century, the terra-cotta figures have been dubbed the Eighth Wonder of the World.

According to historical records, the tomb was similar in grandeur to those of the Egyptian pharaohs. According to Chinese legend, all the laborers involved with constructing the tomb were killed after completing their work to prevent them from telling anyone about the secrets and treasures that lay within. The thousands of terra-cotta soldiers, most of them perfectly preserved, stand guard outside the emperor's tomb. They are housed in three separate wooden vaults. In the first vault archaeologists discovered over 6,000 soldiers and their chariots. The second vault contained 1,400 cavalrymen, horses, and infantry; the third vault, 70 figures. Because human sacrifice had been outlawed by the time Shih Huang Ti ruled, his people buried these statues with the emperor instead of sacrificing real humans and animals to accompany him to the afterworld.

What makes the terra-cotta army particularly fascinating is that each figure's facial features are intricately, and individually, carved. Each statue differs from the one next to it, leading some to speculate that the figures were based on real people. All of the soldiers wore helmets and armor and carried weapons, including swords, crossbows, javelins, and bows and arrows. Life-sized horses are also contained in the vault, with each chariot drawn by a team of four. But while Shih Huang Ti is remembered as one of China's most important leaders, he is also remembered as one of its most ruthless.

For thousands of years ancient China consisted of several feudal states, each ruled by its own prince or warlord. Because of China's huge size, its people have always been incredibly diverse, and the independent warlords were unwilling to recognize anyone as the supreme ruler of the land. As a result, the various states frequently warred with each other, fighting over land and resources in order to increase their power over their neighbors. It would take a

Because human sacrifice had been outlawed, thousands of terra-cotta soldiers were buried in the tomb of China's first emperor, Ch'in Shih Huang Ti. Each statue was so intricate that the facial features of no two soldiers are alike. The tomb and the soldiers were discovered by a farmer looking for water and is often called the 8th Wonder of the World.

teenage prince to unite the country and change the course of Chinese history forever.

Ying Cheng was born in 259 B.C. in the state of Ch'in. He was just 13 years old in 246 B.C. when his father died and he ascended to the throne. From the beginning, the young ruler had one burning ambition—to unify the country and end the constant warring between the states. But he had to wait. Because of his youth, the Ch'in state was governed by a regency for eight years until it was agreed Cheng was ready to take power. With the help of his chief adviser, Li Ssu, Cheng wasted no time setting his unification plan in motion. Over the next several years, his armies methodically and soundly set out to conquer Ch'in's neighboring states using any means possible, be it brute military force or bribery. By 221 B.C., Cheng had vanquished all the other states and was finally in the position to fulfill his dream by proclaiming himself the leader of all China. To commemorate the occasion, he took the name Shih Huang Ti, which means "First Sovereign Emperor."

During his reign, Shih Huang Ti made many improvements— roads and canals were built, and he gave his empire a single currency, a standardized system of weights and measurements, and a common written language in an effort to establish cultural uniformity. In addition, he ordered construction of the Great Wall of China. But the emperor also ruled with a brutal hand. To keep order, he imposed tough laws. For example, if a member of a public works team didn't show up at the job site on time, his entire team would be killed. It is little wonder then that several attempts were made on the emperor's life. All failed. Shih Huang Ti constantly worried about his safety and wanted to make sure he was well protected, both in this life and the afterlife, regardless of human cost. Construction of his tomb and the terra-cotta soldiers, which began shortly after he assumed the throne, took an estimated 700,000 workers over 36 years to finish.

While most people suffered in silence, some spoke out against the emperor's heavy-handed way. The emperor's response to criticism was quick and harsh. For example, he had a particular dislike for the teachings of Confucius, which had much to say about governing powers. These teachings set limits on the power of the ruler, stressed the responsibility an emperor has to the people, and stated that extremes, like the kind of excesses Shih Huang Ti displayed, were to be avoided. As a result, the emperor decreed that all Confucian doctrine be erased. In an attempt to stamp out potential dissent, he also ordered his officials to burn any books that did not agree with his methods—he feared that subjects who read them would become corrupted and start rebelling. These books included the histories of all the former states except Ch'in, folk collections of poetry, and articles and books written by people associated with schools that were known to disagree with the emperor. Even more shocking, a year later he arrested some 400 Confucian scholars and had them buried alive.

Ironically, the first emperor's dynasty ended after a few years; despite Shih Huang Ti's efforts, the teachings of Confucius not only survived but thrived in the centuries that followed. Each new generation embraced the simple but powerful philosophy envisioned by a man who had not lived to see his ideals so appreciated.

Chinese Dynasties

FYI
For Your Info

Shang (c. 1600–c. 1100 B.C.)
Considered by most scholars to be China's first true dynasty, the Shang is famous for its bronze work, including vessels, weapons, and chariot fixtures. The period is also noted for its jade carvings and woven silk. Other advances include an early writing system and the first Chinese calendar.

Chou (c. 1100–221 B.C.)
The Chou, the longest dynastic period in Chinese history, is considered the classical age of China, during which Confucianism and Taoism were developed and many literary classics were written. Other advances include written laws, a money economy, and the use of iron.

Ch'in (221–206 B.C.)
This short but pivotal dynasty saw Ch'in Shi Huang Ti unify all of China, and it gave the country its name. During Shi Huang Ti's oppressive rule, laborers began work on the Great Wall and the emperor's tomb, which was filled with thousands of clay soldiers. Its most enduring achievements were a standardized written language and uniform weights and measures.

Han (206 B.C.–A.D. 220)
The Han Dynasty is notable for the incorporation of Confucian ideals into government. During this time porcelain was produced and Buddhism was introduced. The dynasty was briefly interrupted (A.D. 8–23) by the capture of Wang Mang.

Three Kingdoms (A.D. 220–280) and Six Dynasties (A.D. 220–589)
A long period of disunity and civil war marks this time. Buddhism gained popularity, Taoism became more established, and tea was discovered growing in the south of China.

Sui (581–618)
Following years of unrest, China was reunified and a centralized government reestablished.

T'ang (618–907)
Territorial expansion resulted in increased trade with foreign countries. Buddhism reached the height of its influence. There were many great artistic achievements in painting, sculpture, and poetry. Printing was developed, including the printing of the first paper money.

Five Dynasties and Ten Kingdoms (907–960)
After Tatar tribes moved in from the west, China suffered more unrest and civil war.

Sung (960–1279)
During this period of great social and intellectual change, Confucianism once again gained favor. Tea and cotton became primary crops, and gunpowder was used in the military for the first time.

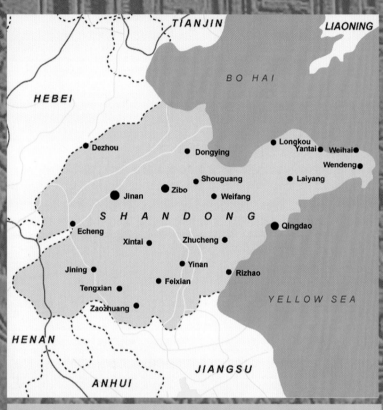

Shandong Province is considered the birthplace of Chinese civilization. It is the site of the first known Chinese city, where the earliest known example of Chinese writing was found and where the pottery, porcelain, and silk industries were first established. Shandong is also the birthplace of Confucius.

CHAPTER
TWO

A HUMBLE BEGINNING

A young man should serve his parents at home and be respectful to elders outside his home. He should be earnest and truthful, loving all, but become intimate with humaneness. After doing this, if he has energy to spare, he can study literature and the arts.[1]

Confucius was born in 551 B.C., the year of the rooster. His family lived in the city of Chou in the state of Lu, which is located in present-day Shandong Province. His father was a general named Shu-Liang Ho, who was already in his 60s and had eight other children from two other wives—but all daughters. When Confucius's 17-year-old mother Yan Zhengzai became pregnant, she prayed she would give Ho the son he had always longed for, and when Confucius was born, there was a great celebration. He was given the name K'ung Ch'iu (*Ch'iu* means "the hill"), because at birth he had an unusual lump on his head. The name Confucius would come many years after his death, when Jesuit missionaries Latinized the name K'ung Fu-tzu, which is Chinese for "Master K'ung," or "Teacher."

Although Confucius's family were commoners in Lu, many years before they had been wealthy aristocrats in the state of Sung, where one of his ancestors, K'ung Fang-shu, had been a duke. Their political rivals had successfully overthrown the family, forcing them to flee to Lu for their safety.

When Confucius was just three, his father died, leaving his young mother to raise him on her own in poverty. Because his parents had not been married when he was born, Confucius was often treated with disdain by other people. He ignored the slights, and even as a child exhibited a deep interest in spirituality. He could often be found play-acting temple rituals.

Because he lived so long ago, not many exact details are known about Confucius's youth. We do know a lot about what life was like during the Chou Dynasty, the historical period during which Confucius lived. At that time, China was made up of a number of feudal states, each ruled by its own leader; there was no single Chinese leader. The kings and nobles of the time lived in lavishly decorated homes and palaces made of brick with tiled roofs. Ornate gardens and landscaping often surrounded the nobles' homes. Among the aristocracy, horseback riding was very popular.

However, most of the people never got to experience such wealth. Most of the population were poor peasants who scraped out a living by farming. Their life was very hard. During the summer, they lived in temporary homes made of bamboo branches located close to the fields. In the winter they moved back to their permanent homes, which usually had just one room and was made of mud. Few peasants could afford furniture, so families sat and slept on the dirt floor.

Although at the time bronze was plentiful and was used to make everything from drinking cups and candlesticks to military weapons, peasants used primitive stone and wood tools. In a feudal system, in exchange for being able to live on the land and cultivate

China is famous for its sculptures, such as this bronze lamp. The earliest known use of bronze in China occurred during the Shang Dynasty, which dates back to 1600 B.C. The early people of China used the metal to make weapons, daily tools, and sacrificial vessels.

it, the peasants had to give the local lord part of the food they grew in addition to gifts, such as wine or silk. They were also expected to pitch in and help whenever the lord needed to have work done on his house or to have local roads or bridges built or repaired.

One of the few bright spots for peasants was the annual spring festival, during which young people, once they were in their mid-teens, would go to meet other people their age. The goal was to find a wife or husband. Regardless of whether a person was a peasant or an aristocrat, nothing was more important for the Chinese than having a family. Confucius agreed with this. As he grew up, he was ever more devoted to the concept of family. He developed definite ideas on the responsibilities everyone had to his or her relatives, particularly older relatives and ancestors.

Confucius grew up in a time of much political upheaval. Because China had a feudal system, warfare was common between states as they jostled for power and land. The state of Lu seemed to be particularly vulnerable. Although the populace was generally artistic and educated, it was a small state without much military might. There was also a lot of internal strife, with three predominant families competing to be the leaders of the state. Assassinations and other crimes such as bribery were not unusual. Then, as the number of aristocrats increased, the feudal system was unable to create enough governmental positions, so "lower aristocrats," or *shih*, who had been educated and cultured, suddenly began to find themselves in poverty alongside the peasants. Confucius was born into a family considered *shih*.

Confucius had an enthusiastic love of learning, but he and his mother lived very modestly. Peasants were not allowed to pursue an education. Confucius was determined to find a way to receive some learning. When he was about 15 years old he went to work for a nobleman. This gave him the opportunity to travel to the imperial capital and study classical Chinese writings, and to become versed in music and sports. He was particularly fond of fishing and even in his youth showed the sense of fairness that would later be the hallmark of his philosophy. When he fished, for example, he didn't use a net, which some believed gave the fisherman an unfair advantage. Confucius earned a reputation as an unfailingly polite young man who had deep respect and appreciation for traditional ways and the ancient laws of China. Confucius was also considered quite tall for his day and physically strong, so he was an impressive figure.

When he was 19, he married a girl from the state of Sung, a marriage that had been arranged by his mother, and they soon started a family. Needing money, Confucius accepted a job running a grain store for the house of the governor of his district, Baron Ji, where Confucius became known for the fairness of his measures.

Wooden statues of Confucius and his wife, Chi-Kaun, who were married when he was 19 years old. They had three children together before separating four years later. It is believed these statues were created by one of Confucius' followers named Tzu Kung, although their current whereabouts is unknown.

The following year he was promoted to oversee the public lands and fields for the nobleman. It was while holding this position that Confucius's son, Le (or Bo Yu) was born. He and his wife would also have two daughters. But the marriage was not a happy one, and after four years, the couple separated.

Instead of looking for a new wife, Confucius immersed himself even more into studying the old ways. Before long he would find himself facing an opportunity to share his knowledge with others.

The Great Wall of China remains one of the most impressive achievements in human history.

At more than four thousand miles long, it is the longest structure ever constructed.

Built to keep invaders out and to separate warring states, the Great Wall was constructed over a period of two thousand years and remains one of the most popular tourist destinations in China.

Great Wall of China

FYI
For Your Info

As the longest structure ever built, the Great Wall of China is considered one of the greatest construction achievements in history. It crosses northern China from the east coast to the central part of the country. Its sheer size is almost unimaginable. It is approximately 4,000 miles long, which is more than the distance from Los Angeles to New York. Even more amazing is that it was made entirely by hand.

The purpose of the Great Wall was twofold. Starting as early as 600 B.C., the Chinese began building walls along their borders as a way to both keep out foreign invaders and to establish boundaries between warring Chinese regions.

The emperor credited with initiating construction of the Great Wall is Shih Huang Ti of the Ch'in dynasty, who ruled from 221 to 210 B.C. His idea was to connect the already existing older walls with sections of new wall as a way to prevent the Mongols from attacking his empire from the north, an area where very few people lived at the time. It was also a way to keep his own people from leaving to become nomads.

The dimensions Shih Huang Ti wanted for the wall were very specific. It was to be six horses wide at the top, eight horses wide at the bottom, and five men tall. Every one hundred yards, the workers were to build watchtowers two stories high. From there, sentries could keep an eye out for invaders. At the top of the wall, a roadway paved with three layers of brick connected the watchtowers. The roadways were wide enough to hold ten soldiers side by side.

The military was in charge of overseeing the project, and it used whatever manpower could be found. It is estimated that a million people, from teachers to convicts, were rounded up and sent north to help build the wall. It was brutal labor, with laborers forced to work day and night, using dirt, stone, and bricks. The punishment for complaining or trying to run away was being buried alive. Countless Chinese laborers spent the rest of their lives working on the Great Wall, and so many of them are buried in the Great Wall it has often been called the Long Graveyard. But the Great Wall was so strong that the Mongols did not threaten China again for more than one thousand years. Construction continued on the wall through several dynasties, with the last improvements made during the Ming Dynasty, between A.D. 1368 and 1644.

Today, although much of the wall is in ruins, it is still large enough that it can be seen by astronauts orbiting Earth. But contrary to popular legend, the Great Wall is not visible from the moon.

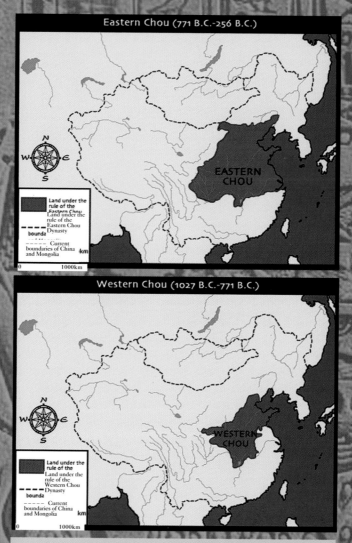

Eastern Chou (771 B.C.-256 B.C.)

EASTERN
CHOU

Land under the
rule of the
Eastern Chou
Land under the
rule of the
Eastern Chou
Dynasty
bounda
Current
boundaries of China
and Mongolia km

0   1000km

Western Chou (1027 B.C.-771 B.C.)

WESTERN
CHOU

Land under the
rule of the
Land under the
rule of the
Western Chou
Dynasty
bounda
Current
boundaries of China
and Mongolia km

0   1000km

The Chou Dynasty is divided into two eras.
The first three centuries are called the
Western Chou Dynasty, and archeologists
regard the population from this era in this
region to be classified as Stone Age
people. The Eastern Chou Dynasty was
marked by a blossoming of Chinese culture
in areas of philosophy, ethics, and politics.

CHAPTER
THREE

EMBRACING TRADITION

Reviewing what you have learned and learning anew, you are fit to be a teacher.[1]

When his mother died in 527 B.C., Confucius buried her next to his father, then went into a long period of deep mourning. After this time of reflection, he began his career as a teacher. But it was not academic subjects that interested Confucius; it was inner knowledge and how that could be used to enhance a person's character. He also yearned to see people, especially rulers, adopt better morals and more compassion.

Looking around him, Confucius was overwhelmed by what he saw as moral chaos and a complete disregard for China's traditional values. Crime was rampant, with robberies commonplace in the countryside and the murder rate rising in the cities. The rich lived ever more extravagantly, while peasants were literally starving. Government officials were blatantly corrupt. The marketplaces were filled with overpriced goods, and many scholars couldn't find work.

All the upheaval and uncertainty made Confucius nostalgic for olden days, when the people of China had lived in peace with one another. Confucius wasn't the only one who sought a way to deal with the social and political problems of his day. But he was unique in that he believed that for peace to be achieved in his time, it was necessary to reinstate the spirituality and practices of the ancient emperors, such as the early Chou Dynasty leaders Wen and Wu. As Confucius's personal philosophy evolved, he concluded that the answer to these eternal questions lay in *li*, the Chinese word for courtesy. Confucius thought that the ideal society could only be achieved by establishing rules based on strict morals that would teach responsibility. He also believed that returning to traditional beliefs, such as ancestor worship, was important. The ancient Chinese believed that after death, a person became a god who watched over their living descendants and interceded with more powerful divine beings on their behalf. Thus, the living would worship their ancestors out of respect and the belief that they were being looked after.

Once his official period of mourning his mother was over, Confucius began attracting some students eager to hear his thoughts about the principles of honorable conduct and good government. A few of his students, or disciples, compensated Confucius, either with food or goods or money. But Confucius would teach anyone with a hunger to learn, regardless of their ability to pay. As the number of his followers grew, so did his reputation, and he became widely known as a man who revered Chinese ideals and traditional customs. He became an adviser to Duke Chao, who also embraced Confucius's teaching.

When Confucius was 33, Duke Chao arranged for Confucius to visit Luoyang, the imperial capital of the Chou Dynasty, to see the temple and to study ancient traditions and ceremonies. While there he also met Lao-tzu, who at that time was in charge of the Imperial Museum and Library but who would later be known as the founder of Taoism. Like Confucius, Lao-tzu was known to be a great thinker. But unlike Confucius, Lao-tzu believed that people needed to focus on the world around them and the harmony found in nature; he thought Confucius's preoccupation with ancient rites was pointless.

Lao-Tzu was a popular thinker of his time and the founder of Taoism, a philosophy that believes people should focus on the world around them in order to better understand how to be in harmony with the universe. Taoism promotes meditation and contemplation as ways to achieve this enlightenment.

According to tales of the encounter, which were recorded long afterward by followers of Lao-tzu, the meeting was strained. As Confucius was leaving, Lao-tzu gave him this advice: "I have heard that rich people present people with money and kind people present people with advice. I am not rich, but assuming I am kind, so I am going to present you with a piece of advice: A man who is brilliant and thoughtful is often in danger of his life because he likes to criticize people. A man who is learned and well read and clever at arguments often endangers himself because he likes to reveal people's weaknesses and faults. No matter whether you serve your parents or your country, do not be too self-centered, do not only think about yourself."[2]

Typically, Confucius was too polite to make a retort, but it was possibly in reaction to the meeting with Lao-tzu that upon passing

Luoyang, sometimes called the Ancient Capital of Peonies because of the flowers that grow there, is considered the home of Chinese Zen Buddhism and is where the famed Shaolin Temple was built in 496 during the Northern Wei dynasty.

the temple in Luoyang he noted a statue depicting a man with his mouth clasped shut. On the back was the inscription, *The ancients were guarded in their speech, and like them we should avoid loquacity [dicussion]. Many words invite many defeats. Avoid also engaging in many businesses, for many businesses create many difficulties.* "These words are true, and commend themselves to our reason," he said to the students with him.[3]

However, Lao-tzu's words may have been prophetic. Twenty-five years later, someone did attempt to assassinate Confucius.

Having no more business in Luoyang, Confucius then returned to Lu, but his stay would prove to be short. Duke Chao had lost a power struggle with two other lords and fled Lu for the neighboring state of Ch'i. Confucius followed the duke into exile and was given a position working as the secretary to Baron Gaozhao. He again gained the respect of those around him, including Ch'i's Duke Jin, who considered giving Confucius some land. But Duke Jin's advisers were against the idea and talked him out of it. Because Confucius was so dedicated to ancient ceremonies and rituals, some people worried that his belief system would be too difficult for the average person to master because it required too much effort and study; others didn't want their modern customs curtailed. After Duke Jin admitted to Confucius, "I'm sorry I'm too old now to be able to put your doctrines into practice,"[4] Confucius left Ch'i and returned to Lu.

In 511 B.C., Duke Chao died in exile. Confucius decided that he no longer wanted to work in government and turned all his energies to studying and teaching. When people heard the news, many wanted him to teach their children. Confucius accepted everyone who came to him with a desire to learn, and thereby became the first man in the history of Chinese education to start a private school.

One of his favorite themes was to teach his students about the importance of loving their neighbor and the need for leaders to love their subjects. One day he and a group of students were out walking when they passed a woman crying near a grave. Confucius sent one of his students to ask what was wrong. She told him how her father and son had both been killed by wild tigers. When asked why she didn't move someplace safer, she replied that despite the danger posed by wild animals, she stayed because the local ruler was fair and just. When he heard her answer, Confucius told his students: "My children remember this—oppressive government is fiercer than a tiger."[5]

After years of unsuccessfully trying to instill moral values within government, Confucius was changing China one student at a time.

Confucius Said

The teachings of Confucius: literature, conduct, loyalty, and trustworthiness.

子以四教、文、行、忠、信。*

Confucius said, "Do not be concerned about others not appreciating you. Be concerned about your appreciating others.

子曰、不患人之不己知、患不知人也。

Confucius said, "The gentleman understands righteousness, the petty man understands profit."

子曰、君子喻於義、小人喻於利。

Confucius said, "In serving parents, make suggestions tactfully, and if your aspirations are not pursued, still respect and do not disobey, bear burdens and do not complain."

子曰、事父母、幾諫、見志不從、又敬不違、
勞而不怨。

Confucius said, "During your parents' lifetime, do not journey afar. If a journey has to be made, your direction should be told."

子曰、父母在、不遠遊、遊必有方。

Confucius said, "Men live with honesty. The dishonest live, spared of fortune."

子曰、人之生也直、罔之生也幸而免。

Confucius said, "The gentleman studies literature extensively, is tempered by the rites, and is unlikely to go astray."

子曰、君子博學於文、約之以禮、亦可以弗畔矣
夫。

Confucius said, "Learn as if behind, and still be afraid of losing what has been learned."

子曰、學如不及、猶恐失之。

*Indicates chinese written version for each saying.

Chinese Language

Chinese, which belongs to the Sino-Tibetan family of languages, has seven major language groups: Yue, more commonly called Cantonese; Kejia (Hakka); Xiang (Hunanese); Min; Gan; Wu; and Mandarin, which is the largest group and is the standard official language in mainland China and Singapore.

The Chinese language is monosyllabic, and intonation is part of a word's pronunciation, meaning the definition of a word is determined by whether it is said with a high-pitched or low-pitched tone. If your voice rises when it should have fallen, you could end up saying a completely different word than you meant to. All Chinese languages and dialects have tones, but Mandarin has one of the simplest systems, consisting of five basic tones, in contrast to Cantonese, for example, with nine contrastive tones.

Ironically, although more people speak Chinese than any other language in the world, because of the phonetic diversity within the language, many people who speak one dialect cannot understand other dialects. Someone from a city in northern China, for example, might not be able to speak to someone from the south. However, since the written language is the same everywhere in China, they could communicate by writing down what they wanted to say.

Written Chinese is not based on an alphabet like English or any of the other European languages. In fact, there is no such thing as an alphabet in China. With alphabets, the individual sounds of the language are represented by letters. Individual letters, by and large, have no particular meaning until they are joined with other letters and can be read or pronounced as a group. Chinese writing, on the other hand, developed as a system in which each symbol represents a concept or idea.

| heart | jade | love | brave |

One of the best things about alphabets is that there aren't that many letters to memorize. However, there are over 50,000 characters in the Chinese language. The average person needs to know about 6,000 characters for everyday use, and it takes most Chinese students several years to learn them.

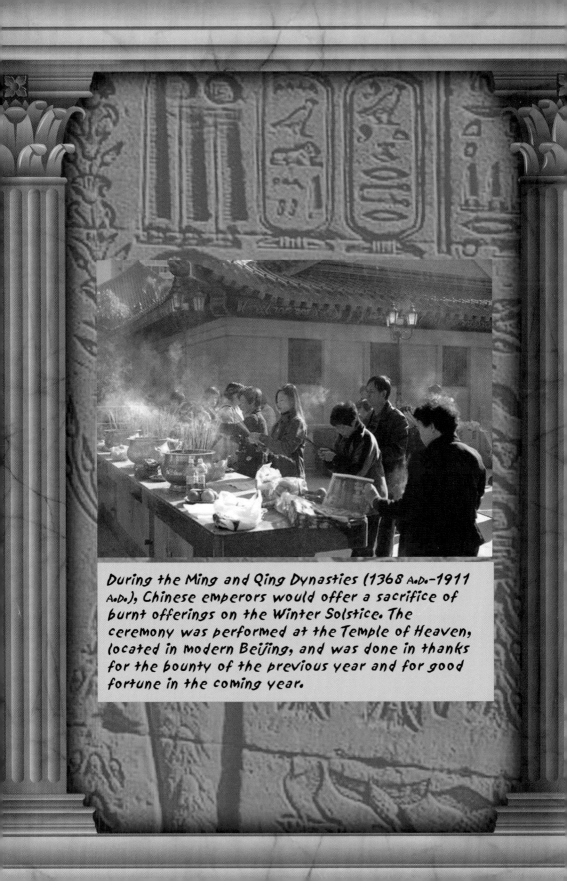

During the Ming and Qing Dynasties (1368 A.D.–1911 A.D.), Chinese emperors would offer a sacrifice of burnt offerings on the Winter Solstice. The ceremony was performed at the Temple of Heaven, located in modern Beijing, and was done in thanks for the bounty of the previous year and for good fortune in the coming year.

CHAPTER
FOUR

THE WANDERING YEARS

There are three common mistakes made by those who are of rank:
(1) To speak when there is nothing to be said; this is imprudence.
(2) To be silent when there is something to be said; this is deception.
(3) To speak without paying attention to the expression on the person's
face; this is called blindness.[1]

Duke Chao's successor was Duke Ding, and the political unrest continued under his rule. When Confucius was about 50 years old, Duke Ding appointed him as magistrate of his city, and the teacher suddenly found himself back in political service. After a year, the town was running so smoothly that Confucius was promoted to Secretary of Public Works, and then later he became the Grand Secretary of Justice. During an official visit by the Duke of Ch'i, Confucius's devout adherence to traditional ways so impressed the visiting leader that, as a goodwill gesture, he returned three areas of land to Lu that had previously been taken in conflicts.

In 496 B.C., during Duke Ding's 14th year of rule, Confucius was promoted once again, this time to Prime Minister of Lu. Finally he was in a position to put his ideas of political reform into action. After just a few months in office, Confucius had so increased order in the state, including dramatically reducing crime, that other states grew concerned that Confucius might use his influence to stage coups, or takeovers, of other states. Some officials of Ch'i, the nearest state, thought the best strategy would be to make Lu an ally; in other words, they thought they should join forces to protect each other from outside threats. But others wanted to try to undermine Confucius's moral influence over the officials of Lu.

Those seeking to undermine him sent the duke and local barons a gift of over one hundred horses; they also sent 80 female dancers to entertain them. The leaders were so enthralled with the dancers that they neglected their official duties, much to Confucius's disappointment. The last straw was when the duke forgot to perform a ceremony called the Sacrifice to Heaven, which was performed on the winter solstice, or first day of winter, when burnt offerings were presented at an altar. The ceremony was a prayer for a prosperous new year. Disillusioned, Confucius left Lu and began a period of traveling through China that would last many years. He wanted to find another opportunity to implement his ideas on how to govern, but instead he frequently found himself unwelcome. Though he was a fair and just administrator, he was also so exacting that it was difficult to live up to his exceedingly high standards.

His first stop was the state of Wei, where Duke Ling welcomed him as if he were a foreign dignitary. At first the duke showed no inclination to employ Confucius in any way, but he changed his mind, deciding he might learn something from Confucius about how to govern effectively. He offered the teacher a stipend, or payment, of 60,000 bushels of rice, which is what his salary had been in Lu. Needing the food, Confucius agreed. In the end, his stay in Wei lasted only 10 months. Other officials of the duke's court were jealous of Confucius, and he believed they were plotting against him. Confucius moved on, heading to Ch'in.

A qin *is a seven-stringed musical instrument that can be traced back three thousand years. In Imperial China, nobles and scholars were expected to learn to play the instrument because it was believed music both elevated the human spirit and enriched the soul. Confucius was considered a master of the* qin *and played it everyday while dancing with his disciples.*

While traveling through the state of Ch'in, Confucius had a frightening experience. Mistaken for another official from Lu who had been guilty of cheating people, Confucius was arrested. His students feared for his safety, but Confucius stayed calm. He told them: "Since King Wen died, I kept the most knowledge of the moral tradition. If it be Heaven's will that this moral tradition should be lost, later generations shall never again share in the knowledge of this tradition. But if it be Heaven's will that this tradition should not be lost, what can the people here do to me?" [2] Eventually, Confucius was set free, and he returned to the safety of Wei.

At Wei, Confucius was restless, and before long he was back on the road, traveling from state to state with a number of his students. Often, when he would stop and recite ancient odes or poetic verses, he would sing them and accompany himself on a *qin*, which is a stringed instrument similar to a zither. Confucius reportedly made a practice of dancing with his disciples every day, because in his time, music was considered to have great social significance. "It is by poetry that one's mind is aroused; it is by ceremony that one's character is regulated; it is by music that one becomes accomplished," Confucius once noted.[3]

Confucius was buried in his home town of Ch'u-Fou. A year after his death, in 479 B.C., his cottage was converted into a temple in his honor. The buildings comprising his temple were restored after being destroyed during a past uprising by Taiping rebels.

Duke Ding died in 495 B.C. and was succeeded by Duke Ai. Three years later, Baron Huan, who along with Ding had disappointed Confucius for missing the religious ceremony those many years prior, was also very ill and still felt bad for not living up to Confucius's expectations. He also believed that had Confucius stayed, Lu could have grown into a mighty power. He told his heir, Baron K'ang, that he wished Confucius to be offered the position of prime minister. After Huan's death, Baron K'ang was prepared to fulfill his dying wish when K'ang's brother stopped him. Instead he suggested K'ang appoint one of Confucius's disciples. That way they would get someone with moral integrity but not have to deal with Confucius himself.

Hearing that one of his students had been appointed prime minister was a sign to Confucius that it was time to go home. He finally returned to Lu; he was 67. He no longer sought public office and devoted his remaining years to studying and teaching.

Confucius Forrest is the largest and oldest family cemetery in China.

Today Confucius Temple encompasses 49 acres and is the burial place for Confucius and his descendants, who are buried under mounds enclosed in a wall. The path leading to Confucius's tomb is lined with animals and guardians.

Of the three major beverages consumed globally—tea, coffee and cocoa—tea is consumed by the largest number of people on earth. It has been an important export for China for over one thousand years. Tea is grown as an agricultural crop in at least twenty provinces.

Although processing tea has become more mechanized, the work of harvesting is still done by hand. It is a slow process with a skilled picker only able to gather a little over a pound of green tea leaves in a day.

In Chinese culture, serving and drinking tea has become a kind of art form. Tea rooms across the country are packed with people enjoying their daily tea rituals. Although tea was originally drank because of its perceived medicinal value, it is now consumed for flavor and as a shared communal experience.

The History of Tea

The modern term *tea* derives from early Chinese dialect words—such as *Tch'ai*, *Ch'a*, and *Tay*—used to describe both the beverage and the leaf. According to Chinese legend, over four thousand years ago, in 2737 B.C., lived a Chinese emperor named Shen Nung. One day while traveling, he stopped to rest beneath a wild tea tree. Shen Nung, who was also a scientist, had issued an order that all citizens should boil water before drinking it, as a precaution against disease. As his servant was boiling water, a leaf from the tree dropped into the water, turning it brown and emitting a pleasant aroma. Shen Nung decided to take a sip of the concoction and was delighted with its refreshing qualities. Thus began the national Chinese obsession with tea.

From the beginning of its popularity, tea was believed to have healing powers, a belief based in fact because tea has very high levels of vitamin C, which helps prevent diseases. It wasn't until the Sui Dynasty (A.D. 581–617) that the Chinese began drinking tea mostly for its taste as opposed to its medicinal benefits. It was also during this time that tea was used as currency, or a type of money. China would trade tea, pressed into small cakes, with its neighbors in exchange for a variety of items including horses and wool. These tea cakes continued to be used as currency in the far reaches of the country even after the introduction of paper money.

During the T'ang Dynasty (A.D. 618–907), tea wasn't just a beverage. It became an essential part of Chinese spirituality, particularly after A.D. 800 when poet Lu Yu (715–803) wrote the first definitive book on tea, the *Ch'a Ching*, which means "The Holy Scripture of Tea." Lu Yu equated tea service with the same harmony and order that controlled the universe. After his book was published, Lu Yu was worshiped as a kind of tea divinity, attracting students to his tea-based philosophy and sought out by the emperor as a consultant and friend. Tea service became a kind of art form. Elaborate tearooms and teahouses were built so that people could enjoy tea while expanding both their social horizons and spiritual awareness.

The tea favored by the Chinese was green, or unfermented, tea. Fermentation is the process during which chemicals in the tea leaf combine with oxygen in the air, resulting in tea with different qualities, such as a stronger taste or darker color. The black tea produced in China was fermented and manufactured entirely for export, specifically to nomads in the north. Some historians believe the Western taste for black tea happened by accident after Europeans received a cargo of tea that had fermented because of an exceptionally long voyage. Believing this was the tea the Chinese drank, Europeans developed a taste for it that continues to this day.

One of several portraits of Confucius painted by Hong Kong artist Peter Mong. Although it's hard to tell from this image, one of Confucius's most notable physical characteristics was his height. Some historians estimate Confucius, whose father was also much taller than the average Chinese man of the time, could have topped out at 6'6".

CHAPTER
FIVE

AN ENDURING LEGACY

I dare not claim to be a sage or a humane man. But I strive for these without being disappointed, and I teach without becoming weary. This is what can be said of me.[1]

Despite his notoriety, toward the end of his life Confucius worried that he had not accomplished much. He felt he had failed to establish true political reform and wanted to leave something of value for future generations. He began researching the religious, ceremonial, and historical affairs of the Hsia, Shang, and Chou dynasties. He wrote down his findings in *Book of Spring and Autumn*, a historic chronicle that spanned a dozen dukes of Lu, from the beginning of Duke Yin's rule in 722 B.C. to the 14th year of Duke Ai, 481 B.C. He told his disciples, "The future generations shall understand me through this book, and they shall criticize me on the basis of this book as well."[2] Confucius also edited the *Book of Songs*, after he personally sang every one of the 305 songs, accompanied by the *qin*, to make sure the book represented the original ancient music style.

When Confucius died in 479 B.C. at the age of 72, he could only have dreamed that his philosophy would one day become the cornerstone of Chinese government and society. Although he was underappreciated during his lifetime, after he died, his teachings took on an almost magical life of their own.

Over the course of his teaching life, it is estimated that Confucius taught around three thousand students, dozens of whom went on to become noted government officials or scholars. It is through those students and disciples that Confucius's school of thought not only lived on past his death but became China's fundamental code of behavior. After his death, in order to preserve his teaching, Confucius's students wrote down all the dialogues they had with him. Over time, they also amassed everything they could that recounted how he solved problems and the various situations in which he had found himself. Eventually, this collection of Confucius's life and work was put together in a compilation called *The Confucian Analects*.

Many of the analects, or teachings, are very familiar to us, such as "What you don't like done to yourself, don't do to others,"[3] similar to the Christian Golden Rule. Most of the analects of Confucius deal with acting in a responsible or sensible manner. Some are simply good advice: "Expect much from yourself and little from others and you will avoid incurring resentments,"[4] and "If you make a mistake and do not correct it, this is a real mistake."[5]

His overall goal was to groom people to carry themselves with grace and to act with integrity. Confucius felt that each true gentleman—which included women—must possess five qualities: integrity, righteousness, loyalty, altruism, and *jen*, which is a respect for all living creatures, or a respect for life. Moderation was also a fundamental key to achieving virtue. According to Confucius,

Buddhism, a philosophy that became a religion, was founded by Sidhartha Guatema, born around 563 B.C. in India. Like Confucius, Sidhartha preached non-violence, compassion, and the importance of personal enlightenment. Although Buddhism fell out of favor during the Sung Dynasty, because it was viewed with suspicion as a "foreign" religion, today over 500 million people follow some form of Buddhism.

maintaining harmony and balance by staying within limits was a true path to personal and spiritual fulfillment.

Although Confucius was revered by many, it wasn't until the Han Dynasty, under Emperor Wu (ruled 141–87 B.C.), that his teachings and ethics were adopted as official Chinese ideology. After that, Confucian values were used to maintain law and order. Scholars would travel into the farmlands to lecture on the importance of such Confucian values as respect for parents, loyalty to government, and keeping in one's place in society. While to some that might seem to promote conservative thought and social castes, and to inhibit free thinking, Confucius also stressed the importance of *ren*, which is love or kindness. He believed *ren* was the foundation and source of all virtues. As China's first private educator, Confucius believed his role was to train young men for government service by molding their character, because it was his conviction that society should be ruled only by those with integrity.

After the end of the Han Dynasty (A.D. 220), Confucianism fell out of fashion for several hundred years as Buddhism's influence spread across China. Then during the Sung Dynasty (960–1279), there was a backlash against Buddhism, which was seen by many as

As Buddhism's influence spread, Confucianism fell out of favor for several centuries. But during the Sung Dynasty, the teachings of Confucius enjoyed a new appreciation. People once again embraced his ideals, but in a modernized way known as Neo-Confucianism. Pictured here is a recreation of a Sung Dynasty-era village.

a foreign religion. Part of the resulting reforms was a return to Confucian tradition, but in a modernized, reinterpreted version that was called Neo-Confucianism. Suddenly, the *Analects* and the Confucian concept that concern for society and government are closely connected with personal ethics were once again studied.

Although it is very much based on a certain moral code, Confucianism is not a religion the way Judaism or Catholicism is. It is a social code of behavior intended to show people the right way to act and to be more responsible to society, friends, family, and self. A person could be Buddhist or Jewish or Christian and still follow the principles of Confucianism.

Confucius's grave is located at Ch'u-Fou. It is found by passing through a magnificent gate and walking down a cypress tree-lined path. As if to make up for all the times officials ran him out of their states, nearby is a number of memorial tablets, representing several Chinese dynasties, intended as homage to the man who has been China's incomparable national teacher.

Every year on the anniversary of Confucius's birthday, September 28, The Confucius Temple in Taichung holds a ceremony at dawn to honor his teachings and memory.

The Confucius Temple in Beijing, Kong Miao, is the largest in China honoring the philosopher outside his hometown of Ch'u-Fou. The Temple now doubles as the Capital Museum, which is home to an exhibit about the culture and history of Beijing.

FYI

For Your Info

Astrology is an ancient belief that human nature and the future can be divined, or predicted, based on when you were born, and that your birth date plays a factor in your personality. Western and Chinese astrology are similar in that they both use 12 signs to define basic categories of personality. But where Western astrology believes the placement of the planets within the zodiac is the basis for these attributes, Chinese astrology believes the attributes are based on nature.

Each Chinese sign has a different animal name and corresponds to a period equivalent to one Chinese calendar year—which is not the same as the 365-day year we use in the West. Chinese years run in a repeating cycle of 12 animal years, always presented in the same order, starting with Rat and ending with Pig. Five 12-year cycles equal 60 years, which is considered a Chinese "century." According to the Chinese calendar, we are currently in the 78th century, which will end in 2044.

The reason Chinese astrology is based on the characteristics of animals has to do with the fact that China was traditionally an agrarian, or farming, culture. Chinese philosophers believed that life is a balance between opposites, called yin and yang. Yin represents cool, soft, and feminine. Yang represents hot, hard, and masculine. The Chinese used animals associated with farming and pasture life as a metaphor for this balance and for the cycle of life because so many people were familiar with these animals. For example, the year of the Ox, which is traditionally slow-moving and hard, is offset or balanced by the year of the Rat, which would be fast-moving. People born in these years are likewise assigned similar traits.

Here are the 12 years of the Chinese calendar and the general characteristics those born under the signs are believed to share:

Rat	aggressive and talkative	Horse	independent and practical
Ox	hardworking	Goat	needy
Tiger	impulsive and charismatic	Monkey	entertaining and generous
Rabbit	nonconfrontational	Rooster	resourceful and bossy
Dragon	festive and healthy	Dog	loyal
Snake	unselfish	Pig	naive and hates to say no

Chronology

(All dates B.C.)

551   Confucius born in the state of Lu, which is now the province of Shandong

548   Father dies

532   Confucius marries

531   Enters the service of a noble family as superintendent of parks and herds

528   After producing a son and two daughters, Confucius and his wife separate

527   Mother dies

525   Begins to teach

518   Meets Lao-tzu

501   Begins his political career; under Duke Ding he is first appointed building minister, then justice minister of Lu

496   Promoted to prime minister of Lu; disillusioned, goes into exile from Lu and travels across China

495   Arrives in the state of Wei

493   Huan T'ui attempts to assassinate Confucius

484   Returns to Lu at the age of 67; spends next four years editing old traditions

479   Dies at the age of 72

Timeline in History

(All dates B.C.)

2680	Pyramids are built in Egypt.
2205	Hsia Dynasty is founded.
c. 1900	China begins to use bronze.
c. 1250	China imports war chariot.
c. 1200	Earliest inscribed oracle bones are made.
1045	Chou feudal system is initiated.
c. 1000	Cuneiform writing is used in Babylonia.
c. 850	Greek poet Homer is born.
753	Rome is founded.
c. 650	Some Chinese states begin minting coins.
563	Siddhartha Gautama, founder of Buddhism, is born in India.
560	Lao-tzu (Li Erh), founder of Taoism, is born.
551	Confucius is born in Lu.
499	The Chinese begin work on the 1,000-mile-long Grand Canal.
490	The Battle of Marathon is fought between Persians and Greeks.
c. 475	Warring States era begins.
470	Socrates is born in Athens.
460	Hippocrates, called the father of medicine, is born in Greece.
221	China is unified under its first emperor, Ch'in Shih Huang Ti.

Chapter Notes

CHAPTER ONE   THE FIRST EMPEROR
    1. *Analects*, 1:5—http://www.hm.tyg.jp/~acmuller/contao/analects.htm.

CHAPTER TWO   A HUMBLE BEGINNING
    1. *Analects*, 1:6—http://www.hm.tyg.jp/~acmuller/contao/analects.htm.

CHAPTER THREE   EMBRACING TRADITION
    1. *Analects*, 2:11—http://www.hm.tyg.jp/~acmuller/contao/analects.htm.
    2. "The Life of Confucius," http://www.e-graviton.com/existence/gurus/
analects2.html.
    3. R. K. Douglas, "Rise of Confucius, the Chinese Sage: Part I: Early Teachings,"
History of the World, January 1, 1992.
    4. "The Life of Confucius," http://www.e-graviton.com/existence/gurus/
analects2.html.
    5. R. K. Douglas, "Rise of Confucius, the Chinese Sage: Part I: Early Teachings,"
History of the World, January 1, 1992.

CHAPTER FOUR   THE WANDERING YEARS
    1. *Analects* 16:6—http://www.hm.tyg.jp/~acmuller/contao/analects.htm.
    2. "The Life of Confucius," http://www.e-graviton.com/existence/gurus/
analects2.html.
    3. "Confucius Not Only Said It, He Played It on the Zither," April 28, 2000—
Associated Press, as quoted on http://www.crystalinks.com/confucius.html.

CHAPTER FIVE   AN ENDURING LEGACY
    1. *Analects,* 7:33—http://www.hm.tyg.jp/~acmuller/contao/analects.htm.
    2. "The Life of Confucius," http://www.e-graviton.com/existence/gurus/
analects2.html.
    3. *Analects*, 15:23—http://www.hm.tyg.jp/~acmuller/contao/analects.htm.
    4. Ibid., 15:14.
    5. Ibid., 15:29.

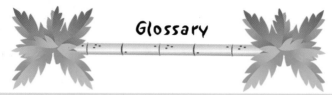

Glossary

ancestor	(AN-ces-ter)—someone from an earlier generation; for example, a parent, grandparent, or great-grandparent.
ancestor worship	(AN-ces-ter WUR-ship)—the belief that after death, a person who watches over their living descendants and intercedes on their behalf with more powerful divine beings. People would worship their ancestors out of respect and the belief that they were being watched over.
bronze	(BRONZ)—a metal made from copper, tin, and lead.
Buddhism	(BOO-dizm)—a religion founded in India in the sixth century B.C. that was introduced into China around the first century A.D. Buddhism promotes enlightenment (freedom from suffering), which is achieved through a life devoted to moderation, morality, and meditation.
Confucianism	(kon-FYOO-sheh-nizm)—a philosophy of life developed by Confucius. It stresses the proper relationships in society, such as between father and son or subject and ruler.
dynasty	(DIE-neh-stee)—a succession of rulers from the same family or line; a family group that maintains power for several generations.
emperor	(EM-per-er)—the supreme monarch of an empire.
feudal system	(FYOO-dul SIS-tem)—a political system in which, in exchange for land, people give part of their produce, or their services, to the local leader, often called a lord.
Han	(HAHN)—the indigenous peoples of China; also, the name of one of the Chinese dynasties.
Mongols	(MAHN-gols)—Generic term for a number of Inner Asian tribes that were united by Genghis Khan in 1206.
nomad	(NO-mad)—someone who moves from place to place, usually seeking pasture for herds of grazing animals.
peasant	(PEH-zent)—someone in the class of people who work the land, usually for someone else.
philosophy	(feh-LAH-seh-fee)—pursuit of wisdom; also, a belief system.
porcelain	(POOR-seh-lin)—a fine, hard, pearly white ceramic, baked at a very high temperature.
regency	(REE-jen-see)—a person or group of people who govern a kingdom for a sovereign who is either underage, absent, or disabled in some way.
Taoism	(DOW-izm)—a philosophy of life founded by Lao-Tzu. It drew on nature as a guide.
terra-cotta	(TARE-eh CAH-tah)—Baked clay, used for architectural features and ornaments, vessels, and sculptures.

For Further Reading

For Young Adults

Allison, Amy. *Life in Ancient China. The Way People Live Series*. Farmington Hills, MI: Gale Group, 2000.

Barrett, G. W. *Ancient China*. Marjorie Reeves, ed. Reprint. White Plains, NY: Longman Publishing Group, 1969.

Confucius. *Analects* (D. C. Lau, trans.). Middlesex, Eng.: Penguin Books, 1979.

———. *Confucius: Confucian Analects, the Great Learning and the Doctrine of the Mean* (James Legge, trans.). New York: Dover Publications, 1971.

Freedman, Russell, and Frederic Clement (illus.). *Confucius: The Golden Rule*. New York: Arthur A. Levine, 2002.

Reid, T. R. *Confucius Lives Next Door: What Living in the East Teaches Us About Living in the West*. Vancouver, WA: Vintage Books, 2000.

Rowland-Entwistle, Theodore. *Confucius and Ancient China*. Danbury, CT: Franklin Watts, Inc., 1987.

On the Internet

The Analects of Confucius
http://www.hm.tyg.jp/~acmuller/contao/analects.html

Chinese History for Beginners
http://www.asterius.com/china/

Confucius—A Biography
http://www.confucius.org/lunyu/edbio.htm

Confucius and Socrates: The Teaching of Wisdom
http://www.san.beck.org/CONFUCIUS1-Life.html

History for Kids
http://www.historyforkids.org/learn/china/philosophy/confucius.htm

The Internet Public Library
http://www.ipl.org.ar/cgi-bin/ref/litcrit/litcrit.out.pl?au=con-318

The Life of Confucius
http://www.e-graviton.com/existence/gurus/analects2.html

Stanford Encyclopedia of Philosophy
http://plato.stanford.edu/entries/confucius

Works Consulted

Berling, Judith A. "Confucianism." *Focus on Asian Studies*, Vol. II, No. 1, *Asian Religions*, Fall 1982, pp. 5–7. As quoted on http://www.askasia.org/frclasrm/readings/r000004.htm. Copyright Ask Asia, 1996.

Brooks, E. and A. *The Original Analects*. New York: Columbia University Press, 1998.

"Confucius Not Only Said It, He Played It on the Zither," April 28, 2000—*Associated Press*, as quoted on http://www.crystalinks.com/confucius.html

Creel, H. *Confucius*. New York: Harper, 1949.

Douglas, R. K. "Rise of Confucius, the Chinese Sage: Part I: Early Teachings." *History of the World*, January 1, 1992.

Fingarette, H. *The Secular as Sacred*. New York: Harper, 1972.

Knoblock, J. *Xunzi: A Translation and Study of the Complete Works*. Three Volumes. Palo Alto, CA: Stanford University Press, 1988, 1990, 1994.

Lau, D. C. *Confucius: The Analects*. Harmondsworth: Penguin, 1979.

Nivison, D. *The Ways of Confucianism*. Chicago: Open Court, 1996.

Waley, A. *The Analects of Confucius*. New York: Vintage Books, 1938.

Index